The Love Songs
of Late Capitalism

The Love Songs
of Late Capitalism

Martin Rowson

Smokestack Books
1 Lake Terrace,
Grewelthorpe,
Ripon HG4 3BU

e-mail: info@smokestack-books.co.uk

www.smokestack-books.co.uk

ISBN 9781739772253

Smokestack Books
is represented by
Inpress Ltd

for Katy and Luke, as a final wedding present
and, as always and forever, for Anna, Fred & Rose

These are just the weeds
That grow between the slabs,
The stubby grass breaking out
Between the cracks in the pavement art.

Contents

Stop Feeling Sorry for the Dead

Stop feeling sorry for the dead
We have to die that others can start living in our stead
And most of us still end up dying cosily in bed
Stop feeling sorry for the dead

And stop feeling sorry for the youth
They're young and dumb and gullible, and here's the damning proof:
A lot of them end up as old as us – ain't that the truth?
Stop feeling sorry for the youth

And stop feeling sorry for the brave
Who bumptiously lead squads of blameless cowards to the grave
And then greet you from a balcony with a brief curt dismissive wave
Stop feeling sorry for the brave

Stop feeling sorry for the strong
The macho generalissimo who'll right your every wrong
By insisting it's the unstrong scum who were guilty all along
Stop feeling sorry for the strong

Stop feeling sorry for the state
Freemarket fascists want to close it down and leave you to your fate
But it still will rob and jail and kill you and lend a helping hand too late
So stop feeling sorry for the state

Stop feeling sorry for your land
The weather is atrocious and the scenery quite bland
And it's overrun with total arseholes neither glorious nor grand
Stop feeling sorry for your land

Stop feeling sorry for the wise
Their every great utopian scheme turns to shit before our eyes
That they're dumb and useless as the rest of us lot's no surprise
Stop feeling sorry for the wise

Stop feeling sorry for the meek
Though the Earth as an inheritance is looking fairly bleak
They forfeited our sympathy when they turned the other cheek
Stop feeling sorry for the meek

Stop feeling sorry for the rich
The fact that they both shit and die is obviously a bitch
But them being greedy psychopaths is a truly lousy pitch
Stop feeling sorry for the rich

Stop feeling sorry for the sick
They'll die or they'll recover. That's basically their shtik
And half the beds in every hospital contain a complete and utter prick
Stop feeling sorry for the sick

Stop feeling sorry for the sad
Often they're sad because they've just done something really bad
So foully irredeemable it drives God and all her angels mad
Stop feeling sorry for the sad

And stop feeling sorry for your gods
That they give a shit about a wanking kid's against the odds
And anyway they're only in your heads you stupid sods
Stop feeling sorry for your gods

And stop feeling sorry for your side
That loses every time because you're so self-satisfied
Though blaming everybody else clearly leaves you sanctified
But stop feeling sorry for your side

Oh, and stop feeling sorry for yourselves
Getting upset about all that stuff in books on all those shelves
Or because in the latest Hobbit film they've miscast the fucking elves
Stop feeling sorry for yourselves

And stop feeling sorry for the poor
They've had so much of your pity they can't stomach any more
Just give the fucks some money and then I'll show you to the door
And stop feeling sorry for the poor

And stop feeling sorry for the dead
The meek, the sick, the rich, your gods, yourselves, the underfed
Save your pity and get furious and make a better world instead
And stop feeling sorry for the dead

Demarcation

Whenever I go clambering from my rut
    I obviously deserve the cold shouldering
And resentful sideways glances over
    Both their own & others' shoulders
I'll be receiving on full beam
    From the pack of comedians, poets, novelists & painters
        hugging walls to blank me,
A massive thinks bubble
    Tethered like a great grey Zeppelin above their heads
    Its fat flat flanks festooned with words of fire, silently
        burning:
'Don't look, but Leopold Fuckoffski just minced in,
The carpetbagging showboating piece of shit'.

Which by and large I reckon
    Is simply as it should be
For no one clasps clear demarcation
    Closer to their breast than I,
And each time that I hear how
    Another much-loved TV comic's
Published their new novel,
    A poet's painting water colour still lifes
Of their sadness, a painter's
    Smeared themselves in sticky gobs of sonnets
Or another novelist is doing stand-up on the Fringe,
    A never-ending funeral cortège commences once again
    Processing through my heart,
    Its sullen pallbearers grinding their stubby teeth
Down into dust.

Because I clearly know
        A baddish fairy breezed up at my birth,
Swaying just a tad too obviously
        And balancing her champagne flute atop my crib
With slightly too much deliberative care,
        Doing her bit of business with her scuffed and cracking
                handbag
Cramming back in cascades of burning rabbit fur,
        Bus tickets, bar bills, strangers' keys,
Tranquillisers, empties & cigar stubs,
        Before pausing to think a bit,
Then narrowing her damp vermilion eyes,
        Spitting in my face & drawling
        'You'll be a cartoonist, cunt.
        Don't step out of line and
Be thankful for small mercies.'

It's like a longlost brother once said to me,
        So drunk that he could hardly speak,
'If you wern ma brother you'd be
        Jus another drawin' faggot,'
Like the tiny women in those caves
        Wrangled received reality,
        Painting and retelling it
        In safe mode, 40 thousand years before
The tyrants and the tax collectors forged writing to
                enshackle us,
And hardly any time at all since we'd found speech.

BOYCOTT *THE GUARDIAN*!

BOYCOTT *THE GUARDIAN*!
Because it's changed
BOYCOTT *THE GUARDIAN*!
Because it's changed its font or something
BOYCOTT *THE GUARDIAN*!
Because I wouldn't read that stinking fascist rag in a hundred billion years and why would you want to be anything except just like me?
BOYCOTT *THE GUARDIAN*
Because it's just there on the side so it's easier than having to look for something else to boycott. That make sense?
BOYCOTT *THE GUARDIAN*!
Because otherwise it'll only be boycotted by Tories and non-*Guardian* readers and THEN how do you think you're going to feel?
BOYCOTT *THE GUARDIAN*!
Because everyone in the World immediately does exactly what it tells them to so sinister and fiendish are the ways of the Main Stream Media!
BOYCOTT *THE GUARDIAN*!
Because I once saw it for sale in a newsagent's literally in the same street as a steak house where, and this is literally true, they had SERF & TERF on the menu, and I'm not even making this up!
BOYCOTT *THE GUARDIAN*!
Because if you read it backwards it says Vote Tory Kill Foxes and they pretend it doesn't!
BOYCOTT *THE GUARDIAN*!
Because it reviews restaurants and is therefore dripping with privilege!
BOYCOTT *THE GUARDIAN*!
Because my principles and opinions will be more than adequately reflected and amplified by *The Daily Telegraph*, *The Tatler* and *Horse and Hound* thank you very much I'm sure they will

BOYCOTT *THE GUARDIAN*!

Because secretly we all want Owen Jones to starve
BOYCOTT THE GUARDIAN!

Because I'm SO ANGRY I'm going to burn my bloody house down and I'll start it with this copy of *The Guardian* and then *The Guardian* will be a murderer and an arsonist AS WELL!
BOYCOTT *THE GUARDIAN*!

Because somebody has to
BOYCOTT *THE GUARDIAN*!

Because they won't let you say anything these days!
BOYCOTT *THE GUARDIAN*!

Because the guinea fowl crossed the boulevard to eat some quinoa la-de-fucking-da!
BOYCOTT *THE GUARDIAN*!

Because it didn't say anything nice about my new shoes
BOYCOTT *THE GUARDIAN*!

Because it didn't thank me for the postal-order I sent it for its birthday
BOYCOTT *THE GUARDIAN*!

Because it wasn't there to hold the hair out of my eyes that time I threw up on the pavement outside the mobile library the morning after that session with the sambuca and benylin shots, remember?
BOYCOTT *THE GUARDIAN*!

Because that cartoon of Jeremy's hat is directly responsible for the existence of food banks in this country!
BOYCOTT *THE GUARDIAN*!

Because it stopped a Labour Government being elected by literally sending Polly Toynbee and Jonathan Freedland to block up all the ballot boxes and blow up all the polling stations and chop off all the little orphans' voting hands for fuck's sake!
BOYCOTT *THE GUARDIAN*!

Because they stopped Jeremy turning it into nutritious gluten free vegan veal to feed the 5000, the Tory pigs

BOYCOTT *THE GUARDIAN*!

Because it's a deadly danger to everyone in the vicinity. Run for your lives!

BOYCOTT *THE GUARDIAN*!

Because it's such a load of liberal rubbish they'll make you wear masks made out of it but it'll be too wishy-washy and rubbish and you'll die of Covid as a direct consequence because it forced everyone to vote for this Tory Government at gun point, the guns made out of recycled sandals and the bullets made of lentils, right?

BOYCOTT *THE GUARDIAN*!

Because if you don't they'll compel you to get all the other things you don't want and before you know it you won't be able to move for pre-fab abattoirs and gaggles of Canada geese and life-size blow-up dolls of Dominic Raab!

BOYCOTT *THE GUARDIAN*!

Because basically it's just the *Daily Mail* translated into French and then translated back again, badly

BOYCOTT *THE GUARDIAN*!

Because how are ordinary decent people who are forced to read *The Guardian* like in that scene from *A Clockwork Orange* meant to find the ingredients for a Yotam Ottilenghi Tuscan quiche? Well? You fucking genocidal bastards!

BOYCOTT *THE GUARDIAN*!

Because to be brutally frank it's not the paper it was when I first started telling you to

BOYCOTT *THE GUARDIAN*!

BOYCOTT *THE GUARDIAN*!

BOYCOTT *THE GUARDIAN*!

Because if you rearrange the letters in its masthead and change a few of them, you'll find it spells 'HITLER'.

BOYCOTT *THE GUARDIAN*!

Cliché

Each war, to put it bluntly, is a cliché,
From ranting bombast through to pity's tears,
With dumbness, murder, lies & black denials,
Plus mayhem, waste, futility and jeers,
Blood pulsing through your temples, drained through fields,
The thrill, the fear, the hate, the love, the laughs,
The mawkishness which cuts each way you look,
Monotonous statistics, bashful graphs.

Every war, in short, is just a cliché.
Always will be; always has been too;
Their tropes merely performative show business:
Her child's leg pulped; a medal pinned on you;
A speech to stir defiance or fresh vengeance;
Injustices so ancient we've lost count;
The stark biology of massive trauma;
The way that pus clots in such prinked amounts.

All wars, to ram the point home, must be clichés:
That's the way we know how they'll be waged.
You stretch your purity until the tension
Requires fresh pogroms of the unengaged;
The sublimation of all random people
To hazy myths from whence we might have sprung,
That aging cranks in bunkers can perfect how
The old can wreak revenge upon the young.

This war, in other words, remains a cliché.
If it was me there now I'd howl for blood
At that pathetic cheap hood's crass neuroses,
And how they'd churned my friends into the mud.
I'd want to loose the darkness we all harbour
To fight a darkness of far darker hues.
Freedom, too, is just another cliché.
Clichés are clichés, well, because they're true.

Election Fever

Vote vote vote!
Vote vote vote!
Vote to let the nation note
The candidate on whom you dote!
Quote – 'The People's Choice!' – unquote –
Has offered you free creosote
So that The People get to coat
A fence to keep out every scrote
Who'll grab each of us by the throat
Once they've got across the moat
In a small deflating boat
Through clumpy stuff that won't not float
As corpses tend, you know, to bloat.

Vote vote vote!
Vote vote vote!
Vote vote for the antidote!
The policies their lords promote!
The stirring slogans, learnt by rote!
Their total failure to emote!
Each worthless promissory note
From speeches that they never wrote!
Ignore what their sneers might denote,
The gravy in their gravy boat,
Actions based on anecdote,
The times they've turned their petticoat,
Lusts that shame a billy goat,
How orphans form their table d'hote –
Just vote vote vote vote vote vote vote
That those you hate might then get smote
By the crank who floats your boat!

For it's your voice so vote vote vote!
And it's your choice now vote vote vote!
So earn your salt and vote vote vote!
It's all your fault the way you vote.
The creeps we reap our votes connote,
So hide your head in your capote
Regret will gnaw you like a stoat,
Observing turds who got your vote.
Hands up! Who wants to cut their throat?

Alternatively, tease the mote
Out of thine eye and grab your coat.
Otherwise they'll just scapegoat
Us chumps whichever way we vote.
So vote vote vote vote vote vote vote
Vote vote vote vote vote vote vote!
Or, on reflection, maybe don't.

The Putative Alpha Male is Dreaming of His Triumph

The putative alpha male
       Is dreaming of his triumph,
Of how he'll snap his aging rival's spine!

The putative alpha male
       Is planning his great triumph
And thinks 'In hours all of this is mine!'

The putative alpha male
       Is wallowing in the prospect
Of triumph, graduating from obscurity!

He's considering the ways
       He'll rend his rival's children
To preserve his group's genetic purity!

The putative alpha male
       Bunches both his fists up
And pounds them in a tattoo on his chest!

He thinks about the sex,
       The roaring, feasts and slaughter
He'll grab when all his rivals have gone West!

The putative alpha male
       Is grinning at the triumph
That he'll parade once he's destroyed his foes!

The putative alpha male
       Is savouring the triumph
He'll taste (it's salty) doubling down their woes!

The putative alpha male
      Is pant-hooting his triumph:
The coming cull, the gore, the broken bones!

The cringing, fawning, grovelling!
      Submissive supplication!
The way each vanquished rival now atones!

The putative alpha male
      Is shaking a large thorn bush!
The putative alpha male stamps on the branch!

The putative alpha male
      Is seeing in his mindseye
Their severed heads in one great avalanche!

The putative alpha male
      Will soon be crowned in glory
And all shall worship him! His ochre face!

And if he loses then of course
      It's all good preparation
To train him for the next leadership race.

Peter Hitchens

They say that you crash funerals as your anointed job
And spit into the mourners' faces, catching them mid-sob,
Proving thus the efficacy of your brilliant gob
That brays that you crash funerals as your anointed job.

Indeed, I often look at you in ways you wouldn't wish,
Looking down your nose again and seeming rather swish
And sneering with grand Trotskyite hauteur, 'Oh dear, what pish!
Dolphins, I think that you will find, are actually fish!'

Delete

If you've a view on shit like Brexit
Please don't phone or call round. Text it!
Texting's fast & fun & neat
And I can simply press delete!

And if you think me & Posterity
Require more trans debate Asperity
So greater wisdom can accrete
Once your diatribe's complete
Text me! And I'll press delete.

In fact, all of your fine opinions
On bettering the lives of minions
Through mad solutions most will greet
Like something ferrets might secrete:
Just send a text, both short & sweet
Then I can simply press delete

And if, from close by Plymouth Docks
I'm sexted pictures of the cocks
Of every sailor in the fleet
Announcing they'll come down our street
So they can blow me off my feet
Until their lusts are quite replete
Honestly, I'll press delete

The loudest liberals may beseech
We honour all Freedom of Speech
A truth embedded in concrete
Nonetheless, though bittersweet,
Not Listening also should compete
With other freedoms in retreat
So shout out loud 'Don't soil you sheet
Each time I choose just to delete!'

And when the thunderous voice of God
Rumbles through my dying bod
Reduced to so much rotting meat
Informing me my life's complete,
That I'll be harvested like wheat,
And wound up in a winding sheet,
Sat in Life's ejection seat,
Facing Inferno's sulph'rous heat,
Ready for the mourners' suite,
A turd Existence will excrete:
In short, that I'm about to meet
My Maker (but first meet St Pete) –
Although this may be indiscreet,
I think that even then I'll greet
The Word of God like melting sleet
And so ignore the Paraclete:
A Scriptural text is like a tweet
So in my solipsist conceit
Though this may smack of self-deceit
Just one last time, I'll press delete.

Churchill's Bust

Of course, it takes time to adjust
When you've been seriously concussed
And things are best left undiscussed,
Like how the whole world's got us sussed,
Despite imagining we're robust
We're rotting from the uppercrust,
Our hearts corroding into rust
And just one feeble, foetid gust
From crumbling into tumbling dust...
But are we bothered? Are we fussed?
Of course we're not! You get my thrust?
It's cos we've still got Churchill's bust!
Churchill's bust
Churchill's bust
Two hundred thousand dead is just
Statistics! We got Churchill's bust!
And so what if the toffs encrust
That Union Jack with jaded lust?
Brexit's like Churchill! We got bust!
We got bust
We got bust
Thank fuck we still got Churchill's bust!
Churchill's bust
Churchill's bust
Churchill's bust
Churchill Churchill Churchill's bust!
[Repeat to fade]

Churchill's Statue

In days of old when knights were bold
    They'd joust and cry 'Have at you!'
Machine gun hoods, to grab the goods,
    Routinely rat-a-tat you.
The PLO will strike a blow
    And blithely Arafat you
And even cows, between the ploughs,
    When stressed might well cowpat you.
The cricket pitch can be a bitch
    When dark-skinned chaps 'owzat you
While Russian crooks, to cook the books,
    Expertly laundromat you!
Sarajevo's no place to go:
    Warlords Serbo-Croat you
And at Oxbridge they'll drop a fridge
    From spires to exeat you.
For any thug might pull the rug
    To anonymously splat you
While all your kin would give their skin
    To requiescat you
And some bent Ron in Babylon
    Still yearns to ziggurat you
Or random kids, now on the skids
    Will simply copycat you.
Yet not one dares, despite hard stares,
    TO TAKE ON CHURCHILL'S STATUE
    CHURCHILL'S STATUE CHURCHILL'S STATUE
    TO TAKE ON CHURCHILL'S STATUE

Everything's hateful, so just be grateful
We'll jerk your leash and pat you
And let you see how we stay free:
    IT'S DOWN TO CHURCHILL'S STATUE!
    CHURCHILL'S STATUE CHURCHILL'S STATUE
    DOWN TO CHURCHILL'S STATUE!

And should you doubt this truth, you lout.
Your family will rat you
And firing squads will sort you sods
    AT THE BASE OF CHURCHILL'S STATUE
    CHURCHILL'S STATUE CHURCHILL'S STATUE
    AT THE BASE OF CHURCHILL'S STATUE

The Angry White Man Blues

I woke up this mornin
Dead song birds on my bed
Well I woke up this mornin
That dawn chorus lying dead all round my bed
Yet through the stifflin silence
An angry white man said

'Who woke me up this morning
From my deep dreamless snooze?
Who woke me from my slumbers?
Please mind your ps n qs!
My mind's marked 'DO NOT DEEE-STURB'
With your latest grim news!

'How we're heading to the slaughterhouse,
We're just lambs n rams n ewes
Getting fleeced by our own shepherds!
What care I? Please excuse
Me if I don't wanna get Woke
Up by your snowflake views!

'Let the sandman fill my eyes up
So I'm ignoring all those clues
That the whole world's set for burning
These are facts I simply choose
As my masters count their money
To dismiss as fake news!

Rock me in the arms of Morpheus
As I pick not to refuse
To exercise my freedom
Each Woke joker to abuse:
Whores, queers, slopes, shines n liberals!
Damn! Nearly forgot the Jews!

My Privilege is my Freedom
As every real man knows
My ignorance my wisdom,
To remain comatose!
Don't get woke to wear the Woke Yoke
Now please let me repose.

Rock me in my nice white cradle
Me and my fellow yahoos
Lullabied by reprised lies
To light my short short fuse
Won't get woke to wear your Woke Yoke!
Got those Angry White Man Blues!'

Club Class

The air hostess, mature & kind,
Draws the veil across the aisle
To keep us out of sight & mind
With an apologetic smile.

But up in Club Class, shielded thus
By the Velcro'd curtain's locks
From the sight & stench of us
I wonder – do they yank their cocks,

Piss in each other's mouths, fellate
Businessmen from Amsterdam,
Filthily manipulate
Savage instruments and ram

Their bulbous & bejewelled knobs
Up the anuses of chaps
Off to terminate the jobs
Of thousands in the Ruhr? Perhaps

That couple coupling in row three
Across the seats marked D to F
Who harmonise in ecstasy
In screams above a treble clef

Are in a start-up in AI
Who'll meet investors in Milan
Once past their wild climactic high
Which they're now passing with elan!

And now the ululations drown
Out the engine noise! What now?
The air stewards are dragging down
The aisle a garlanded young cow!

How did those onyx knives get past
Security? Those dark libations
Are not from duty free! Aghast
At strange & foul sets of vibrations

Accompanying the screams & howls
That come from beyond curtains plush,
In Economy our rumbling bowels
Inspire us all to rise and rush

And storm Club Class, those scenes Tiberian
The Five Mile High Club's devotees
Enact in skies Gallic, Iberian,
Teutonic or above the seas

Towards which this plane starts to plummet!
Our forward rush has set askew
Our balance, from celestial summit
To Earth's embrace! The cabin crew

Use billy clubs & scented towels
In vain attempts to calm the room;
Instead they set off louder howls
As we all realise our doom!

The plane crashes! The fuselage
Splits in half just like a gourd!
The front half being by & large
The Club Class section, and aboard

Sit its denizens, now sated,
Laughing as our back half sinks
While we all drown, quite irritated
They're being served yet more free drinks.

Bucket List

I don't want to go to Australia
Nor pierce studs through my genitalia;
Thoughts of thrills on the Zambezi
White-water rafting make me queasy;
I do not wish to waste two hours
At Disneyland or Alton Towers
And Moonlight and the Taj Mahal
Just strike me, frankly, as banal;
As for trying out sky-diving
Or the prospect of arriving
In New Zealand, haunt of kiwi,
I'd rather drink a pint of wee-wee,
Nor would a Caribbean cruise
Get close to starting to amuse.
Won't join the army, seeking glory,
Obviously I won't vote Tory,
Won't lose at roulette in Las Vegas,
Invoke demons with a magus
Swim with turtles off the Chagos,
Get sent 10 million bucks from Lagos,
Or pray to God down on my knees:
I yearn to do not one of these,
Nor visit far exotic places
Wanly to smile at kindly faces,
I don't wish to plan any more
Things I've never done before,
And nor do I, goddam and fuck it,
Intend to plan to kick the bucket.

Although, one day, of course, I will.
And I shall sicken and grow ill,
Burst into flames or something odd,
Or simply get struck down by God.
But then, when I am almost dead
And lying there on my deathbed
Some gurning clown will say to me
In tones of purest idiocy:
'Ooh look! You're dying! There's a twist!
That's one crossed off the bucket list!'

Trip Adviser

When you breakfast with the cunts who put the cunt in
        Countryhouse Hotel
You have to wonder if a single one of them would ever tell
The children who have served them with their granola how much
        they're worth
And how meagre are the scraps the Meek will get inheriting the Earth.

And the cunts who put the cunt in Countryhouse Hotel are sleek and
        tanned
Darker ochre than the panels in their rooms, which each night cost a
        grand
Including of course breakfast, which comes with a small but fresh
        infusion
Of berries & a local spice the colour of a new contusion

And the Cunts that put the cunt in Countryhouse Hotel come
        from afar
For the hip Modern British cuisine & a greasy pummelling in the spa
And a face towel drenched in fennel & a candle scented with some
        myrrh
For the cunts in Countryhouse Hotels are quite divine & never err.

But as the World these cunts have made & own gets nearer to the edge,
That World they've killed with hedge funds which is how these cunts
        have made their wedge,
Will any of them get it in their tanned, toned, tousled blonde haired
        bonces
That the cunts in Country Houses always were among the Earth's worst
        ponces?

The parasites, the scum on top, thieves leeching off the dieting land,
Squandering our health to flaunt their wealth that crumbles into sand,
Oh let the bells of hell and just desserts and endless woe now go yell
Their fates to all the cunts who put the cunt in Country House hotel!

The Clowns, The Crooks, The Cranks, The Chancers, The Careerists, The Charlatans and the Refugee

Once the clowns, the class clowns all the other kids now shrank
back from in Earth-swallowing embarrassment, playpenned my
country and trashed it for a laugh
    I, like many others, began to keen for exile
And when the crooks, their mates, had stripped down the dump of
every last remaining ounce or speck of any value
    I prayed of being saved by being deported
And when the cranks then squeezed the final cloudy drops of
decency from every other single thing round here
    I dreamed of paying up and racing towards the trucks
And then, when after all of that the chancers, in the others' wake,
began to cadge off all of us for just another roll despite having
already blown the lot
    I imagined holding my breath and cramming into the gap
And then when the careerists smiled with patronising eyes and
turned away to laugh again too loudly at the monsters' jokes
    I saw myself sliding down the pebbles on the beach
And when the charlatans at last monopolised the sole remaining
free churned patch of mud – my land – as solely theirs to shit on as
they choose
    I found that I was wading out towards the rubber dinghies
Hideously but helplessly aware that, because accidents of geography
are trumped by politics and we're meant to think that's normal, I
should soon be floating downwards to the dappled seabed, lungs
ballasted with brine,
    Along with all the other exiles from everywhere,
    Displaced by murderous thieves.

Isle of Wight Haikus

Trees are broccoli;
Pale soup floods through the mudflats.
This teatime landscape.

Narrow lanes, small minds;
The thatch neglected haircuts
On lairy young scalps.

The Solent coughs spray;
Waves break like instant coral;
Flags flap like blisters.

Sunshine on white sails
Seduces complacently
With afternoon lies.

Romagna Haikus

Bertinoro's swifts,
Slim arcs of screaming darkness,
Black sickle squadrons

Banshee round towers,
Fast basking murmurations
Planktoning the gnats.

Renaissance vistas
Whitening through focal fields
Sanguinary depths;

Ignorant armies
Clashed by right in clear sight of
Fungible beauty,

Whereas cicadas
Within the magnolias
Jam all frequencies.

Bologna Airport:
Departure gates in Retail,
Unwanted items,

They exiled Design
From this Global Shopping Mall.
Italy's betrayed.

Imagine

Imagine you're a protoplankton at the moment of your death
And the Universe with wild caprice then infuses your last breath
With the sudden gift of consciousness, and with some foresight too
So that first you know you're dying, but also that you now see through
Countless aeons of future time, and likewise through the laid
                                                          down strata
Of rocks piled down to crush you to a goo, just like a
                                                squashed cassata,
Along with all your family and friends until you've all been squelched
By Time and pressure to a greasy gunk, a hydrocarbon belch
Beneath the Earth, where you'll reside in death, near Hell, a
                                                        tacky slime
For vast incomprehensible extents of neverending time.

Though now, of course, you see through Time like glass, and
                                        likewise through geology
To clearly see the future path pursued by subsequent biology
High up above you on the land that pocks through oceans on the crust
Of Earth, and with it humankind, that imago of future dust
Who makes its money, wages wars and lays down strata all its own
By burning up your corpse, your family's too, like it's testosterone,
Ceaselessly grasping godhood by devouring the hecatomb
Which honeycombs the Earth whose surface it infests like
                                                fungal bloom,
A thanatocratic death cult, a necrophagus parasite
Which, like a stupid virus, will destroy its host. And then you might

In the nanoseconds prior to your own last consummation
Smile reflecting that each schmuck who's queuing at a petrol station
Is, despite their hunch that they're recruits for some angelic host,
Exactly like the rest of Life on Earth: eventually toast,
Destroyed by oil executives, share prices, clowns and thieves
                                           who knew
That burning up the bodies of the long dead would then kill
                                         them too,
For death's built into life, as a failsafe measure, as a brake,
A mechanism that will, given time, correct each bad mistake
In the case of humans through the suicide of Global Warming.
And then you'll laugh, for in the oceans' depths the plankton
                                       still are swarming.

The Shit Inside My Head

Staggering past 63 is it that astonishing I continue to double-take
    at the shit inside my head?
And frequently I'm blind-sided by quotidian happenstance of
    breathtaking mundanity though everything's been said
And worlds drowned inside raindrops streaming down a
    windowpane conspire to leave me breathless with awe
    conjoined to dread
Though occasionally my prejudices suddenly get ambushed by
    glimpses of osmotic spasms flowing once I am dead
So the dreams that fill the universe behind my flicking eyeballs
    will then inform the dreams of worms my body will have fed,
Meaning they and generations of subsequent ingesters will
    consequently get to share the shit inside my head
Although, by then, the me I deem I'm teasing from the maelstrom
    will be the faintest echo in the shit inside their heads

The Museum of Vague Memories

I spied a traveller from an antique land:
To be precise my own curated past,
Crammed with indexed clutter, thick with dust,
Albeit in the odd display a card,
Handwritten, which explains: 'This exhibit's
Now been binned; it was on loan but crumbled
In visitors' rough, thoughtless hands. Things do.'
I think I'm going to blank this traveller,
Although I spotted him just now, mirrored
In another case, its dusty smeared glass
Preserving sixty years of random trash,
Memories of sunshine on a bus stop,
That kind of crap. I'll run out to the park
Filled with salt statues looking the wrong way.

Left On Hold

Do you still remember when
  They kept the whole wide world on hold
And we sat there waiting months
  Just left out hanging in the cold
Month on never-ending month
  While every week or so a voice
Blamed the volume of our calls
  As if this whole thing was our choice
While they played us scratchy trance
  And ears numbed and hands went dead
Til, eventually, it changed
  To endless days of Simply Red?

And do you remember still
  How hypnotised by their delay
Thought would drain away to leave
  Our reveries the space to play,
To imagine other paths
  To future possibilities
And alternatives took flight
  Each spawning new infinities
Of how to live, what to do,
  A Galaxy of Different Worlds,
Sat there, waiting, left on hold,
  While inside all those knots unfurled?

Then with a cardiac click
  A voice in Bangalore or Bray
Said 'Sorry that you had to wait.
  What can we do for you today?'
Then their flat Call Centre tones
  Announced 'Full Service is Resumed!'
Worlds inside your head collapse:
  Our old, dead one has been exhumed;
The possibilities constrict;
  We're stitched in a tightening suture,
Despatched, packed in a cardboard cage,
  To our claustrophobic future.

Last Night

Last night I dreamed I saw my mum,
Dead since I was ten years old,
A frequent desideratum.
She said to me, 'I know they told
You that I'd died, but ever since
I've just been hiding. Just right here.'
I don't know who this might convince.
I'm pleased, though, that she's made this clear.

Last night I dreamed I met my dad.
He died when I was 44.
It didn't make me feel that sad,
Liaising in the evermore.
Instead we talked of this and that,
His latest news and such and such.
He's moved into a mansion flat.
These are the sort of things we clutch.

I dreamed last night about dead Jon,
Best friends when we were 17.
His brain tumour, he said, was gone
They way they do: it's quite routine.
Apparently they'd found a cure.
He's soldiered on. We duck and dive
In order simply to endure.
I said, 'I'm glad that you're alive.'

Last night I dreamed about the home
We sold once everyone was dead
Now ticking like a metronome.
My step-mum let me in and said
'Hello.' My father's many clocks
Tick-tocked there near the prime meridian.
I loved her too. We spoke ad hoc
About the boring and quotidian.

Each night behind our twitching eyes
We navigate an inner realm,
Tombola'd memories the prize,
Some other fucker at the helm.
They'll say the world beyond those eyes,
Honeycombed with shame and glory,
Is all that counts. Once more, their lies
Will only tell you half the story.

.

Autumn Days Like These

Autumn days like these
Don't make me think
Of mists or rotten fruit
But throw me back in Kodachrome
To first shit days at brand new schools
And nervous fear, anxiety,
Heat, frantic positioning
Affirming that eternal truth
The Past's Another Country but
It's a Penal Settlement
From which escape's impossible.
We all remain, forever, on parole.

The Softness of our Daughter's Heart

The softness of our daughter's heart
Never fails to break my own
The way she bawls her eyes out at
The nonagenarian's tram seat fixed
On dumb & mawkish tv shows,
The way a cartoon scene can trigger
Yowls of anguish from almost her whole
Lifetime ago, and how she soaked her mother's skirt
Watching her favourite film, *The Little Princess*
Head in lap, when she was roughly 8 years old.

Considering I've watched her flay grown men
With less than seven slashes of her tongue,
I ceaselessly stand back in awe
Of her infinite versatility,
Just another reason why
That girl, now grown up too,
Is bloody wonderful.

Kiss

I do not even need a kiss
To help refuel the ceaseless bliss
I get from being near you. This
Neverendingly makes me hiss
With joy, just like a serpent
Slithering into Eden.

Self Medication

Last night I self-medicated
Too liberally. Anxiety
Spitefully had liberated
A fear of raw sobriety.

Unfiltered thoughts from darkest realms
Had partied hard all afternoon;
The kind of guest who overwhelms
With savage bants, then steals your spoons.

And all because you've gone away
For just five nights. Those founding stains
Of separation always stay
For far too long, yanking my chains.

Grief, adoption, bereavement haunt
My soul with wraiths I daren't admit
Who break in anyway to taunt
And drag me down into the pit.

Though with a glass of wine or three
I threw them out, slammed shut the door
Like all of us, intemperately,
Find ways to gild the primal flaw.

The flaws, though, get amalgamated
Into a carapacing scar
And thus, calloused, we're separated
From one another, kept afar.

That separation is decreased,
Though all of us are fogbound ships,
Because we can reach out at least
To brush each other's fingertips.

The Rapture

The book had bored me as books often do,
To the point my eye'd been caught instead
       By my bedside light
A big black hammerheaded maw that rears
On sleek black mamba coils all set to strike.
       It screamed a white
Baroque and blinding Godbeam in the dark;
Perpendicularly stabbed the bedroom's black
       As if from Heaven's height.
For dancing in the beam were motes of dust,
Specks swirling ever upwards just like souls
       In rapturous delight.

And then you lowered your own, better book,
Half looked my way & said, suspicious, 'What?'
       And I said 'Look!'
Although some mordant fancy all about
Ecstatic souls beneath my bedside light
       Wouldn't, I knew, hook
Your interest. The flecks of dust still rose,
The specks of us, our moulted air dried meat
       Time tends to undercook.
And you resumed your reading, turned a page
And sent those soulmotes spinning down to Hell:
       A blast of judgement from your book.

I do not hold with sky gods, nor with skies
Crammed with dupes who won't lie but gulp lies
     That Death sends their souls flying.
Transfiguration won't transfix me either
And nor have I concluded my real birth
     Proceeds upon me dying.
And all in all the holy sacred texts,
Like many books will merely bore me more
     However hard they're trying
To translate me and you as sacrifice
No more than dust bowl harvests for some gods,
     Sacramentally calcifying.

You read. I stared. Dust settles through the house.
We slough some more that blizzards to the skies
     To dust the mountaintop.
And on we crumble; the books flake into scabs,
The bulbs burn out, the dust piles up in drifts.
     Perhaps a teardrop
Will blacken (not for long) a patch of dust
Until it dries again and we two, mingled,
     Start to hop
And float and rise in Rapture and we'll dance like dust
And flash and spark in Stardust until Light and Time
     Just stop.

The Love Songs of Late Capitalism

The minicab declutches at the lights,
Descants a Doppler shush and jolts to rest;
The heating in this car is turned too high;
The air-freshener cloys, chemically sweet,
Sways in gagging half-arcs from the mirror,
The oblong void against the windscreen's fringe
Where raindrops stream sideways in coral reefs,
Are pinpricked into gold refracted globes
Or speckle white to pixilate shut shops
Then smear off with a thud from wipers wired
With clenched intensity like mods on speed.
A thwack, a screech, some spray, a brutal sweep,
A Sisyphean mind-fuck written small,
Obliteration as eternal grind.
Then the lights, a greasy splodge, are changing
As music throbs out of the radio,
Music that is older than the driver,
Basses lisping, lung-hawkingly deep,
The trebles harmonising with the ashtray,
A self-contained cacophony on wheels,
Capital Gold – Smooth, Magic – playing louder
The Easy Listening soundtracking our lives
That stays holding your hand long after midnight
And leaves my thoughts to segue in the dark.

The isle has always been too full of noises,
A sickle in an oak grove, rhythmic screams,
A lyre plucked, lies retold as plainsong,
Songs of murder yelled down drunken halls,
Chants in chantries, chancing deathly changes,
Full aisles muffling psalms of anxious pleas,
Feudal furrows shielding famished fieldsongs,
Coughs from dust blown in from stolen meadows,
The bawl of pistons orchestrating Hell.
The gold's percussion counterpoints the sighs,

Haphazard honks of brass grasp at salvation,
Young men in tweeds & cycle clips on raids
To hedgerowed hamlets sack old women's airs,
Anthems, chorales, arias, lovesick ballads;
Echoing dance bands swirl gauche *pas de deux,*
Songs round the piano in an air raid,
Concert party Pierrots down the pier,
Crooners crooning rationed maple syrup,
Songs of yearning grief & cheap pomade,
Genocidal oompah on the bandstand,
Rounds at rallies, rounding on the foe,
Sanitised to sing round guttering campfires,
Rousing roundelays to flay the flagging
Until the time the aisles grew wild with rockers,
Fairground flick knives flashing to the beat
That beats in time with klaxons on the dodgems,
Drowns out the silent screams of brylcremed kids
High on dads' dismay, young lust and danger
While being broken on the Ferris wheels;
The beat of forest drums, beats forgotten,
The beat of fear and night being repelled
Reawakened to reboot the Post War,
Equip the New Age with its potlatch props,
Grave goods for the pyramids of Boomers,
Its scooters, T-Birds, boys' haircuts, their shoes,
For culture wars waged by the rising side
With the heartbeat beat of being human
Expropriated from the mouths of slaves.

The Balls Pond Road's hedgehogging in the rain:
Once Twice Three Times A Lady. 4am
From Tower Hamlet's hissing thoroughfares
The City rises like a sneered affront,
Its hubristic fruit-machine high towers,
Their algorithmic auguries aglow,
Paying jackpot bonuses each second,
Chorused by designer bells and whistles.
The traders homeward long since roared their way,

Leaving the floors to cleaners and machines.
Buff humming tanks glide polishing between
The desks and termini, gilding the guilt,
Varnishing to sterilise the damage
Done the day before, resumed today,
The ceaseless round of pillage and returns,
Prophecy, propitiation, plunder,
Until time, in Swiss watches of the night
To pause, draw breath, get slaves to hose the decks,
The unperceived, the ancillary serfs
Now guiding all those laundering machines
Across the trading floors, like ploughmen trudged
Behind their straining teams, across unyielding
Rock-sewn land, all owned by someone else
Who always, always, always looked away.

Behind shutters hard due north of Shoreditch,
Too late even for inconvenience stores
(The rain's so hard the drunks have all gone home)
Hardened diasporas from everywhere
Beyond the Anglophonic Solipsism
Reach the time of night dreams dissipate,
Displaced by deep defragging sleep. Some scraps
Of previous dreams of former homes still jangle
Above rooms crammed with stock, the cheaper scree
And broken up moraine left by the glaciers
Of Global marketplaces grinding through
And bulldozing new landscapes while pursuing
The paths of least resistance into which
Fresh topographies of mass consumption
And glib geologies are to be crushed;
Dream places lives ago the Europeans
Claimed were undiscovered, Brigadoons
Which unperceived by white eyes stayed dark ghosts
Before we teased them out and made more ghosts,
Places where the trucks and kiosks rattle
With amplified tracks Westerners laid down
When small boys, as they watched the white men leave,

Felt the winds of change ruffle their blazers
And now, as old men, wear tops emblazoned
With Queen's tour dates in 1989
And children squat in shanty towns, in lycra,
Embossed with branded white boy bands' sour pouts,
Uncontacted tribes have traded sweatshirts
For arrow-heads or manioc or skins
And consequently end up advertising
Guns 'n' Roses or, maybe, The Fugees;
The bounty of the sweatshops, holey relics,
Indulgences both pirated and pure,
The ineffectual intellectual loot
Of corporations hawking bored elation,
Snapping on the wristband chains of freedom,
In new colonialisms of pure tat
As I board the midnight train to Georgia,
Born to Run to Galvaston or Nutbush,
Clarksville, LA, Memphis, Nashville, Tulsa,
Songlines mythologising urban blight
And though from here it's five minutes to Dalston,
The radio plays on twenty-four seven,
Day after day, tied onto the tracks
Only interrupted by the ads,
The shilling, spiel, the barking for the heists,
Hard selling commodified rebellion,
Seeking selfish boy singer/songwriters,
New Dylans to revive the slumping shares
By bringing down Bastilles with t-shirt slogans:
8 billion individuals born to swarm.
Near the Tower, and indicating left,
Steady cicada throbs over the songs,
The car is still too hot, just like the World
And the music never ending, like the heist.

See! Quarries of light entertainers piled
In sacrifice appeasing Rock's cruel gods:
In plane or car crash, shot, inhaling vomit,
Or suicide; Nepenthe's pick 'n' mix,

Booze, fast living, bad behaviour, drowning
But always young enough, round 27,
To count as golden children come to dust,
Templating standard Romantic hard-ons,
Blue-jeaned Chattertons, slicked-back haired Keatses,
Shit-faced Shelleys or O'd-ing Christs,
Delicious easy deathfuls of dumb kids
Too high on fame, money and growing up,
Buddy, Ritchie, Jimi, Tupac, Amy,
Jim, Kurt, Sid, Nick, Tim, Janis, Gram, Brian,
Even Elvis dying on the toilet
Undergo tinselled apotheoses
To mount Olympus, squalor washed away,
And sacrament the lie: The Good Die Young.
No gods since the Aztecs' seem this hungry,
Frantically devouring young flesh,
Howling for a Paschendale of pop stars,
Doomed youth designed to go over the top.
Age shall not weary them, nor years contend
With celluloid or vinyl's ersatz aspic
That capture them in blobs now beyond Time:
The Beatles stay The Beatles as they ran
Through black and white industrial decline
That's now cemented in the past; they're present.
Like Ziggy Stardust, Bowie notwithstanding,
Should reek of power cuts and Three Day Weeks
And yet achieved escape velocity
From History's bonds, the Seventies' grey pall,
Transfigured into immortality
And Lenined like Snow White in glassed enchantment
Forever then and eternally now.
Transubstatiating thus, cheap music
Lignifies to tree rings, carbon dating
Exactly memories of time and place,
Evoking more than any hoarded totems –
Snaps and souvenirs, your dead mum's shit –
All those forgotten times we trail like skin scale,
In clouds that haunt like thickening ectoplasm,

Pinpointing memories like ethered moths,
Jerking your leash, a reflex that'll Proust you,
Getting Svengali'd by The Glitter Band,
Just jellyfish in Time's capricious currents.
The only option's worship or despair
Or queuing on your knees towards the tills
Of superstores, with racks of tabernacles
And sepulchres stuffed, stacked up to the skies
Filled with CDs, albums, LPs, downloads
Of packaged troubadours of caught, lean love,
Votive candles flickering rank on rank,
The tallow dripping meatily to sizzle
On cold mosaic floors of Halls of Fame,
Lit to the Trinity, the three-chord riff.

It's late. It's always late, and getting later,
40 years since Marvin Gaye was shot,
But still his voice, like Hamlet's father's, reaches
To me, like a seance in this fug.
The streets are empty as we cross the river,
London's Styx, reflecting Southwark's towers
Mirrored, pointing downwards into Hades,
Filled with the dead who sleep, bat-like, inverted.
The living boogie on. They keep on truckin'.
Stayin' Alive. Keith Richards' bingo wings
Flap at another gala for The Needy
Watched by Presidents and Queens and Kings
Who sway in time to much loved banging classics
About oppression, drugs, sex, blues and rape,
Pastiched by two Dartford boys who spotted
The Delta in The Thames for them to steal
Sixty years ago, though if you fold back
From then the way we turn to then from now,
Those boys would be obsessed with Marie Lloyd.
Mick yowls, his hair inhabiting continua
Divorced in time from what contains his face.
Paul McCartney's mouth, a feline anus,
Mewls words mewled a million times before,

A gerontology of rock and rollers,
Old boys on endless tours singing old songs
In forced communion with men they hate,
Bands of Brothers decayed to Cains and Abels
From decades knocking round and getting old,
Trapped and bored stiff in late adolescence,
Cursed, in shabby reworkings of Dante,
To tour forever Hell's provincial rings
To milk the last drying fungible drop
Of once being Rod Argent or in Mud
In atavistic senicults in Tring
Or Bailey's, Watford for the OAPS
Who hunch with spiders web tattoos across
Their mottled, wrinkled, lesioned once young faces,
Pates too bald or thinning for mohicans,
Anarchy in the UK droning limply
In another singsong in the care homes
While the fallen arches of their idols
Mark their mortality, deteriorating
Into cranks and codgers like their dads,
Mark E Smith recast with 20 woodbines,
Ian Brown van morrisoning crap,
Morrissey jekyll and hyding Farage,
Yet leavening the disappointment seeping
From daring to grow old before they die
Redeemed beyond the peonage of bores
Because their teenage avatars once channelled
The energy of not giving a shit,
Making their mates dance and then feel happy
Back in the time when they were first in love
While Brain Wilson glances at his watch
Halfway through *God Only Knows*, the closest
Any of them got to biting chunks of
Heaven directly from the foetid air.

The Christian skygod, since displaced, allotted
To man a span to live exceeded now
By the Hegemony of Teenage Kicks which
Globalised and monetised the yearning
Of nervous boys and girls who want to fuck.
Back catalogues in warehouses of memories,
Hawking nostalgia, evaporated youth,
Universalising toddlers' dress codes
As Freedom's uniforms, infantilizing
Humanity to sell another song.
For merchants merchandise. It's what they do.
Ghettos of sub-cultures warp to brands;
Elitist and completist, young fans' need
For meaning through belonging twisted round
To opportunities to sell them back
Their dreams in furtive bags of their own shit
Spiked with lines of unquenchable sadness
At recollecting old scuffed leatherette,
Stacked speakers stickier with sweat than beer,
Slimier smoothnesses of mosh pit limbs,
Blissed rictuses and cleaned out fridgidaires,
Composty pagan prog rock comeback tours,
More detestable summer festivals,
Chemical toilets, Glastostomy bags,
Along with the spaced out, intense conviction
That any of this means a fucking thing.
Life's available through ticket agents:
Just psychotropic noises calculated
Like bland deceptive fascisms of sport,
To trigger massive endochrinal rushes
In every shop and restaurant and club,
Grand anthems that sell garbage no one needs,
Aspirational chord changes on games shows,
In madnesses of crowds in massive stadia
Attenuating into tyrants' fanfares,
To make you cheer or weep or shop or kill.

We're in Jamaica Road now, named by slavers
To honour wealth they stole from shackled toil,
Whose 'property', to break the chains within them,
Sang songs they'd smuggled on the ships from home,
Songs their captors eventually then captured
To steal the one last thing they hadn't grabbed,
Then, passed off and repackaged by hucksters,
Trickling down, enveloping the planet
In cauls of sentimental pomp, for sale,
Filling all the gaps between the atoms,
The Disco beats that broke the Berlin Wall
To bring an End to History, then Hope
To move beyond the Neverending Now,
Needily new, requiring fresh worlds
Each week for charts and markets to expand,
Like roaring air from bomb blasts, specks of dreams
Drowned in the flying debris of the cloud
Expanding and expanding beyond bounds
Of pointillistic possibilities,
To blast your ears and take your breath away,
Capitalism's love songs play forever,
Basically just there to fill dead air.
It's easy. Easy like Sunday morning.
I lean forward to the driver, and we speak.

I Wish that I Could Write a Poem

I wish that I could write a poem
People'd read at funerals
To make you sad while your dead dad
Is getting blitzed to minerals
Even though your attitude to dads
Is worse than Goneril's.
I wish that I could write a poem
People'd read at funerals.

I wish that I could write a poem
People'd read at funerals,
Some trite verse won't make things worse
So even Auntie Muriel
Sparks folks' fond chat (the daft old bat)
Amidst the stale profiteroles.
I wish that I could write a poem
People'd read at funerals.

I wish that I could write a poem
People'd read at funerals,
Some stanzas to disguise the cancers
That beat back all those becquerels
And lately did for Uncle Sid,
Ripped to his tits on Demerol.
I wish that I could write a poem
People'd read at funerals.

I wish that I could write a poem
People'd read at funerals,
And thus send Mum to that good night,
That twilight unendurable,
Raging against the dying light
With canons fired by Pachelbel.
I wish that I could write a poem
People'd read at funerals.

I wish that I could write a poem
People'd read at funerals
To awaken at the wake,
With my redemptive doggerel,
The notion Gran went with elan
Just like an East End Criminal!
I wish that I could write a poem
People'd read at funerals.

I wish that I could write a poem
People'd read at funerals;
Disguise with lies the big surprise
That Death is inescapable;
Pretend instead, that though he's dead,
Your Grandad was exceptional.
I wish that I could write a poem
People'd read at funerals.

I wish that I could write a poem
People'd read at funerals
Recited by some surpliced clowns
Breathily liturgical
Or humanists with pious frowns
Pretending to be rational
I wish that I could write a poem
People'd read at funerals.

I wish that I could write a poem
People'd read at funerals,
Some poignant rhymes to rewind Time,
Though such hope is delusional,
So stabbed kids won't end laid on slabs
Just like fucking mackerel.
I wish that I could write a poem
People'd read at funerals.

I wish that I could write a poem
People'd read at funerals
For golden lads and lasses must
(Because all is ephemeral)
Like chimney sweepers come to dust.
We're all of us expendable.
I wish that I could write a poem
People'd read at funerals.

I wish that I could write a poem
People'd read at funerals,
To cousins hemmed in gruesome crems
Along the North Kent littoral
And forge words to show Death's absurd
In my poetastic crucible
I wish that I could write a poem
People'd read at funerals.

I wish that I could write a poem
People'd read at funerals.
I wish that I could write a poem
People'd dread at funerals.
I wish that I could write a poem
They'd read at my funeral.
Anything, Sweet Jesus Christ,
To stop them playing *Angels*.

Afterword and Acknowledgements

The poems you've just read were written over a period of years both before and after the Plague Songs sequence I produced in 2020 during the Pandemic lockdowns. Essentially, they're more of the stuff that tumbles through my mind but will never find a place in the cartoony outpourings of the day job. Indeed, a lot were written by me grabbing some unforgiving minutes when exiled from the drawing board, on trains, round swimming pools or on aeroplanes when there was nothing else to do and, as usual, I found myself incapable of sitting still.

My thanks, as ever, to Andy Croft at Smokestack Books for publishing this, our 8th book together (excluding those of his I previously illustrated). Also to Luke Wright, who continues gigging with me although he's a considerably better poet than I am, and also for looking through the poems and coming up with some suggestions which, this time, I've actually heeded. Likewise, thanks to Patricia Bargh, someone else I've used as a sounding board and who suggested changes I couldn't see; to my agent Matthew Marland; Jon Tregenna, who's already put 'Angry White Man Blues' to music in Vol I of the *Plague Songs* albums we collaborated on in lockdown still available to watch on YouTube; Mike Quille who's already published some of these on the Culture Matters website. I'm also grateful to The Wanstead Tap, The Fisher Theatre, Bungay, The Corn Hall, Diss, *Chartist Magazine*'s Editorial Collective's Annual Dinner, the car park outside Brockey Brewery's Hither Green taproom and Jeff Town's bookshop at The Laugharne Weekend for hosting the first performances of many of these poems. And finally, thanks and love to my wife Anna, to whom several of these poems are addressed and who just about continues to tolerate me wandering hopelessly off piste with stuff like this.

Lewisham, Autumn 2022